Pamper Yourself ...
Pamper Others!

Pamper friends, family or even yourself when you select projects to sew in just two hours or less!

No special sewing skills are required—just the love of sewing. Each project is made from a basic pattern and is easily adapted to reflect your personal style or that of the recipient by adding special embellishments like rickrack, lace, ribbons or buttons.

Who wouldn't love receiving a gift basket full of personally stitched pampering gifts! Just add a few scented creams or sugar scrubs, and you have created a personal spa day. Or select a special bottle of wine and slip it into the Present It Wine Caddy along with a gift card or personal note tucked in the front pocket of the caddy.

I hope these will become your go-to patterns when you need a quick and special gift.

Margaret

Scuff It,
page 14

Meet the Designer

Margaret Travis, owner and designer-in-chief of Eazy Peazy Quilts, is proud of her Ohio-Midwestern roots where learning to sew was part of her family's tradition.

After completing college, she taught elementary school for several years, taking time out to raise her family. Upon rejoining the workforce, she gained experience in marketing and management, much of it in the publishing business.

In 2009, Margaret launched her company, Eazy Peazy Quilts, to design patterns with a whimsical touch. Her designs are suitable for all skill levels and include handbags, accessories and a line of helpful items for the handicapped and household.

In 1996, Margaret moved to Orlando, Fla. where she met a new group of sewing friends to share her love of design and sewing.

Table of Contents

Stow It, page 7

Cozy It, page 10

Carry It, page 29

Soothe It, page 18

Basic Sewing Supplies & Equipment

- Sewing machine and matching thread
- Hand-sewing needles and thimble
- Straight pins and pincushion
- Seam ripper
- Removable fabric marking pens or tailor's chalk
- Measuring tools: tape measure and ruler
- Pattern tracing paper or cloth
- Point turner

- Pressing tools
- Pressing equipment: board and iron, and press cloths
- Rotary cutter, mats and straightedges
- Scissors
- Seam sealant
- Serger (optional)
- Fabric spray adhesive (optional)

Present It

This bag is the perfect gift wrap for a bottle of wine or sparkling apple cider. It is embellished with a pocket for a gift card or a note of thanks to the hostess.

Finished Size

12 inches tall, 11 inches in diameter
Fits standard 10–12-inch-diameter wine bottle

Materials

- 2 coordinating fat quarters A and B
- 18 x 22-inch piece light- to medium-weight fusible batting
- ⅔ yard ⅜-inch-wide grosgrain ribbon
- Walking foot with quilting bar (optional)
- Basic sewing supplies and equipment

Cutting

From fat quarter A:
- Cut one 14 x 16-inch body rectangle.

From fat quarter B:
- Cut one 4 x 13-inch cuff rectangle.
- Cut one 3½ x 8-inch pocket rectangle.

From fusible fleece:
- Cut one 14 x 16-inch rectangle.

Quilting Bag Body

1. Follow manufacturer's instructions and fuse fusible batting to wrong side of 14 x 16-inch body rectangle.

2. Quilt layers together as desired.

Assembly

Use ¼-inch seam allowance and stitch right sides together unless otherwise indicated.

1. Square up quilted body rectangle to 13 x 15 inches.

2. Press ¼-inch to wrong side along one 13-inch side of the cuff rectangle and edgestitch close to pressed edge.

3. Match and stitch opposite 13-inch raw edge of cuff rectangle right sides together with one 13-inch side of quilted body rectangle. Press seam toward cuff.

4. Cut body/cuff piece in half lengthwise to make two 6½ x18-inch pieces. Set aside.

5. Fold pocket rectangle in half right sides together to make 3½ x 4-inch pocket. Stitch raw edges together, leaving a 2-inch opening on one side for turning (Figure 1a). Trim corners diagonally (Figure 1b).

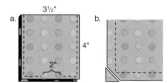

Figure 1

6. Turn pocket right side out. Turn opening seam allowance to inside and press flat.

7. Position pocket centered and 4½ inches up from bottom of one body/cuff piece and topstitch sides and bottom of pocket referring to Figure 2.

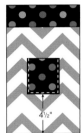

Figure 2

8. Cut 18-inch length of ribbon and fold to mark center.

9. Fold second body/cuff piece in half lengthwise to mark center. Position ribbon right sides together on second body piece 11 inches up from body bottom edge, matching centers (Figure 3).

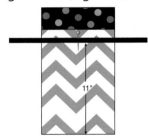

Figure 3

10. Stitch ribbon to bag along center mark. Temporarily pin ribbon ends to bag center away from bag sides.

11. Pin bag pieces right sides together and stitch sides and bottom of bag. *Note: Finish seams with a zigzag, overedge stitch or serger for a finished look.*

12. To box bag bottom, match bottom seam to side seam forming a triangle at corner (Figure 4). Stitch across corner triangle 1 inch from point referring again to Figure 4. Trim seam allowance to ¼ inch and finish seam edge referring to step 11. Repeat on opposite corner.

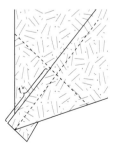

Figure 4

13. Turn cuff down toward wrong side of bag at seam and press. Hand-sew in place along cuff hem.

14. Turn bag right side out and fold cuff down approximately 1 inch.

15. Tuck a gift card, business card or personal note into the pocket for the perfect complement to your gift. ■

Easy Quilting Patterns

If your fabric has a noticeable pattern, you can stitch around or along it, like the zigzag pattern of the sample.

You can also mark 45-degree lines approximately 1½ inches apart across the right side of the bag rectangle in one direction for channel quilting or in opposite directions for a crosshatch diamond quilting pattern. Stitch along the marked lines using a walking foot with or without a quilting bar.

Or simply stitch a random meandering pattern over the entire rectangle.

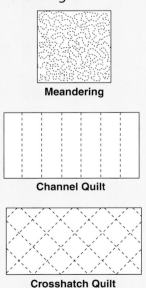

Meandering

Channel Quilt

Crosshatch Quilt

Stow It

Tame the bedside clutter by storing useful items within arm's reach in the four pockets of this bedside caddy. Just insert Stow It between the mattress and box springs. It's also great over the arm of an upholstered armchair!

Finished Size
16 x 24 inches

Materials
- 3 coordinating 44/45-inch-wide lightweight woven prints or solids:
  - ½ yard each of fabric A and B
  - ¼ yard fabric C
- 1 coordinating fat quarter
- 1 yard ⅜-inch-wide grosgrain ribbon
- ½ yard lightweight cotton batting
- ½ yard medium-weight fusible interfacing
- Fabric basting spray
- Walking foot with quilting bar attachment (optional)
- Basic sewing supplies and equipment

Cutting

From fabric A:
- Cut one 18 x 34-inch rectangle for side A.

From fabric B:
- Cut one 18 x 34-inch rectangle for side B.

From fabric C:
- Cut three 2½-inch-wide by fabric width binding strips.

From coordinating fat quarter:
- Cut one 13 x 12½-inch rectangle for pocket.

From batting:
- Cut one 16½ x 34-inch rectangle for body.

From fusible interfacing:
- Cut one 6½ x 12½-inch rectangle for pocket.

Assembly
Use ¼-inch seam allowance and stitch right sides together unless otherwise indicated.

1. Smooth side B wrong side up on flat surface and spray with basting spray following manufacturer's instructions. Smooth 16½ x 34-inch batting rectangle onto B. Spray batting and smooth side A wrong side down on top of batting.

2. Quilt as desired referring to Easy Quilting Options on page 8 for ideas.

3. Square up the quilted rectangle to 16 x 32 inches for caddy body. Set aside.

4. Refer to Applying Mitered Binding on page 9 to bind quilted caddy body with binding strips.

5. Fuse pocket interfacing to wrong side of one half of fabric pocket following manufacturer's instructions (Figure 1).

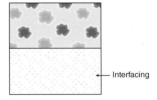

Figure 1

6. Cut a 12½-inch piece of grosgrain ribbon. Position, pin and stitch ribbon piece to the right side of the fabric pocket 5 inches up from the bottom raw edge of interfaced half (Figure 2).

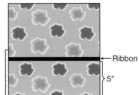

Figure 2

7. Fold pocket right sides together and stitch raw edges together, leaving a 4-inch opening for turning on long side.

8. Trim corners at an angle and turn right side out, gently pushing corners out. Turn opening seam allowance to inside and press all edges flat.

9. Topstitch approximately ⅛ inch from the folded long edge.

10. Position and pin the pocket centered on width of the caddy body on the A side and folded pocket edge 1 inch from a short side as shown in Figure 3.

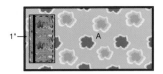

Figure 3

11. Topstitch the stitched pocket side and bottom edges in place referring again to Figure 3.

12. Fold pocket end toward caddy body B side approximately 8 inches and pin in place to make a large pocket (Figure 4).

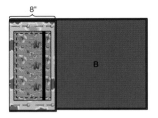

Figure 4

Easy Quilting Options

"Quilt as desired" means just that—you get to choose. If you are a quilter who sews, you will have lots of ideas! If you are a sewer who quilts only rarely or not at all, here are two easy options.

• For a channel quilting design, mark a horizontal or angled line at center of top layer with removable fabric marker or chalk. Layer and baste batting between the top layer and backing. Stitch using a walking foot with a quilting bar in opposite directions working from the center out, following the instructions for the walking foot.
Note: If you are not using a walking foot with a quilting bar attachment, mark lines across the top an equal distance apart with removable fabric marker or chalk for stitching lines.

• For a crosshatch quilting design, mark a horizontal and vertical line or two crossing angled lines at center of top layer. Layer and baste batting between the top layer and backing. Stitch using a walking foot with a quilting bar in opposite directions working from the center out following the instructions for the walking foot.
Note: If you are not using a walking foot with a quilting bar attachment, mark lines across the top an equal distance apart with removable fabric marker or chalk for stitching lines.

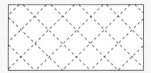

Crosshatch Quilting

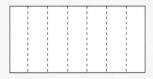

Channel Quilting

13. Stitch close to binding edge to secure large pocket sides.

14. Stitch a vertical line centered, through all layers of pockets to make a total of four pockets (Figure 5).

15. Tie a bow from remaining grosgrain ribbon and hand-stitch to center of pocket ribbon embellishment. ■

Figure 5

Applying Mitered Binding

1. Join binding strips on short ends with diagonal seams to make one long strip; trim seams to ¼ inch and press seams open (Figure A).

Figure A

2. Fold 1 inch of one short end to wrong side and press. Fold the binding strip in half with wrong sides together along length, again referring to Figure A; press.

3. Starting about 3 inches from the folded short end, sew binding to project top edges, matching raw edges and using a ¼-inch seam. Stop stitching ¼ inch from corner and backstitch (Figure B).

Stop ¼"

Figure B

4. Fold binding up at a 45-degree angle to seam and then down even with project edges, forming a pleat at corner, referring to Figure C.

Stop ¼"

Figure C

5. Resume stitching from corner edge as shown in Figure C, down quilt side, backstitching 1/4 inch from next corner. Repeat, mitering all corners, stitching to within 3 inches of starting point.

6. Trim binding end long enough to tuck inside starting end and complete stitching (Figure D).

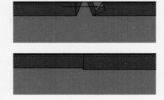

Figure D

7. Fold binding to project back and stitch in place by hand or machine to complete your quilt.
Note: For a stronger final binding seam choose machine stitching. Pin binding and edgestitch or stitch-in-the-ditch from the front of the project catching the binding on the back.

Cozy It

This easy-to-make bed jacket begs to be worn every day. Made from a purchased sweatshirt and embellished with binding, pockets and appliqué, this bed jacket will be your go-to piece when you want to feel comfy cozy.

Finished Size
Your size

Materials
Your size lightweight pullover sweatshirt
Note: *Do not purchase an oversized sweatshirt.*

- Scraps for appliqué at least 5 inches square yellow and green prints
- ½ yard coordinating print
- 7 x 14-inch piece light- to medium-weight fusible batting
- 8 x 10-inch piece paper-backed fusible web
- Tear-away stabilizer
- Basic sewing supplies and equipment

Cutting

From coordinating print:
- Cut three 2½-inch by fabric width strips for binding.
- Fold remaining fabric in half right sides together. Using pattern provided on page 42, cut four pockets.

From fusible batting:
- Cut two pockets using pattern provided.

Assembly
Use ¼-inch seam allowance and stitch right sides together unless otherwise indicated.

1. Prepare one each flower, flower center and leaf appliqué pieces on page 41 referring to Raw-Edge Fusible Appliqué steps 1–3 on page 13 from scraps. Do not remove paper backing at this time. Set aside.

2. Machine-baste ¼ inch and ¾ inch above sweatshirt bottom ribbing to stabilize bed jacket hem.

3. Mark center front of sweatshirt with fabric marker or tailor's chalk (Figure 1). Cut along center front marked line and between bottom row of basting

and ribbing at sweatshirt bottom referring to Figure 2. If necessary, trim bottom edge to straighten, but do not cut through basting.

Figure 1

Figure 2

4. For pockets, follow manufacturer's instructions and apply fusible batting to wrong side of two pockets.

5. Layer fused pockets right sides together with remaining two pockets matching raw edges. Stitch around pockets, leaving a 3-inch opening at pocket bottom for turning.

6. Trim corners at an angle and clip curved seam allowance. Turn pockets right side out gently pushing out corners. **Note:** *Clip curved seam allowances to, but not through, the stitching line to help the curve lay flat.*

7. Turn opening seam allowance to inside and press edges flat. Topstitch ⅛ inch away from pocket curved edge only (Figure 3). Set pockets aside.

Figure 3

8. Refer to Applying Mitered Binding on page 9 to apply binding to center fronts and bottom of bed jacket. Stop stitching several inches from bed jacket neckline and remove from machine.

9. Trim binding length ¼ inch beyond neckline ribbing. Open binding and turn ¼ inch to wrong side; press. Refold binding, pressing if necessary, and complete stitching.

10. Turn binding to wrong side over raw edges and seam line, and pin in place on front close to seam.

11. Stitch-in-the-ditch along binding seam, catching binding in stitching on wrong side of bed jacket. Remove basting stitches around bottom of sweatshirt.

12. Position pockets 1½ inches from center front and bed jacket bottom on both right and left front of jacket referring to Figure 4. Topstitch along all straight edges.

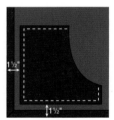

Figure 4

13. Remove paper from appliqué shapes. Refer to the appliqué motif and layer shapes on left front shoulder with center of design 6–8 inches down from neckline at shoulder and 4–5 inches over from center front (Figure 5). *Note: Appliqué motifs usually show a numerical order for layering pieces of the design. Dotted lines will show where the pieces overlap.*

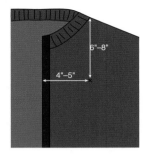

Figure 5

14. Refer to Raw-Edge Fusible Appliqué steps 4 and 5 on page 13 to fuse appliqué pieces in place and machine-stitch around the raw edges using a blanket or zigzag stitch. *Note: Position and pin a square of tear-away stabilizer under the appliqué before stitching. This will make stitching the slightly stretchy sweatshirt easier. Carefully tear away stabilizer when done stitching.* ∎

Raw-Edge Fusible Appliqué

The following instructions are for one type of appliqué technique; refer to a comprehensive sewing guide for other types of appliqué techniques and further details. Appliqué motif shapes are given reversed for this technique.

1. Trace the appliqué motif shapes onto the paper side of paper-backed fusible web, leaving at least ½" between shapes. Cut out shapes leaving a margin around traced lines. **Note:** If doing several identical appliqué motifs, trace motif shapes onto template material to make reusable templates.

2. Follow fusible web manufacturer's instructions and fuse shapes to the wrong side of the fabric as indicated on pattern or in instructions for color and number to cut.

3. Cut out appliqué shapes on traced lines. Remove fusible web paper backing from shapes.

4. Again following fusible web manufacturer's instructions, arrange and fuse pieces to project referring to project pattern.

5. Hand- or machine-stitch around all exposed raw edges of appliqué motif. Some stitch possibilities are machine satin and zigzag and machine- or hand-stitch blanket and running or straight stitch.

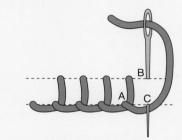

Blanket Stitch

Running Stitch

Scuff It

Soft and comfortable, these slippers are perfect for the spa or bedroom. An antiskid sole with an added layer of cushioning makes for a very comfy shoe. The hook-and-loop closure makes the straps adjustable for a custom fit.

Finished Size
Your size (S, M, L)

Materials
- 1 each coordinating fat quarters:
  tangerine/aqua print A
  aqua print B
- 1 each 12-inch square:
  antiskid gripper fabric
  polyester-covered foam
  heavy-weight interfacing
- 18 x 22-inch piece light- to medium-weight fusible batting
- 2 (2-inch) pieces, sew-in ¾-inch hook-and-loop tape
- 1 yard 1½-inch-wide grosgrain ribbon
- ½ yard tear-away stabilizer
- Walking foot (optional)
- Fabric basting spray
- Basic sewing supplies and equipment

Cutting

From fat quarter A:
- Fold fat quarter in half, lengthwise right sides together, to make a 9 x 22-inch rectangle. Use Slipper Sole pattern in your size, from pattern insert, to cut two slipper soles (one reversed) and four each small and large straps, from pattern insert, referring to Cutting Chart 1. Transfer all markings to fabric.

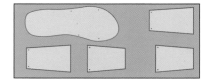

Cutting Chart 1

From polyester-covered foam, heavyweight interfacing & antiskid gripper fabric:
- From each material, cut two slipper soles using the Slipper Sole pattern in your size from the pattern insert. Reverse one sole referring to Cutting Chart 2.

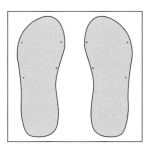

Cutting Chart 2

From fusible fleece:
- Use the Large and Small Scuff It strap patterns from the pattern insert. Fold fusible batting in half lengthwise to make a 9 x 22-inch rectangle. Cut two each Large and Small Straps.

From fat quarter B:
- Cut 2½-inch-wide bias strips to make at least 60 inches when stitched together, referring to Cutting Chart 3.

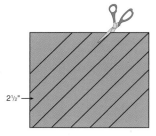

2½"

Cutting Chart 3

From ribbon:
- Cut two each 15-inch and 3-inch lengths.

Assembly

Use ¼-inch seam allowance and stitch right sides together unless otherwise indicated.

1. Layer antiskid fabric, antiskid side down; heavy-weight interfacing; polyester-covered foam and fat quarter A soles, right side up (Figure 1). Follow manufacturer's instructions and spray-baste layers together.

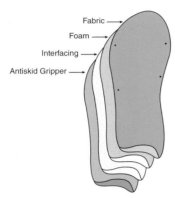

Figure 1

2. Machine-baste through all layers of both slipper soles. Trim layers even.

3. Follow manufacturer's instructions to apply fusible batting to wrong sides of two each large and small straps. ***Note:*** *Remember that you are making a right and left slipper. Keep straps for right and left slipper with appropriate slipper referring to figure drawings and photos.*

4. Layer and pin a fused strap right sides together with an unfused strap. Stitch together leaving the small end of the large strap and the large end of the small strap open for turning, referring to Figure 2.

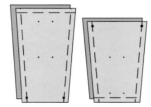

Figure 2

5. Trim corners at an angle and turn right side out. Press flat.

6. Repeat steps 4 and 5 with remaining straps.

7. Position and edgestitch loop side of hook-and-loop tape to the small straps at small circles marked on pattern (Figure 3). Repeat with hook side of hook-and-loop tape on large strap, again referring to Figure 3.

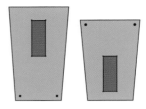

Figure 3

8. Overlap and pin larger strap on top of the smaller strap. Match large squares and circles on straps to slipper sole and pin straps in place. Machine-baste straps in place and trim ends to match slipper sole shape.

9. Stitch bias strip short ends together with diagonal seams to make one long bias binding strip; press seams open. Press one short end of bias strip ¼ inch to wrong side. Then, press strip in half wrong sides together lengthwise (Figure 4).

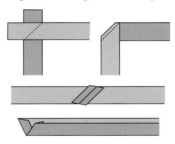

Figure 4

10. Start with folded end at outer edge along outside of sole (not an inner curve); match and pin raw edges of binding to slipper sole. Stitch binding to sole, being careful not to stretch binding as you stitch around the heel; stop a short distance from beginning (Figure 5).

Figure 5

11. Overlap unfolded binding end over beginning and trim length approximately ½ inch beyond the beginning end. Finish stitching binding to slipper sole.

12. Fold binding to antiskid bottom side covering the seam line; pin from top side. Topstitch binding to slipper from slipper top side catching turned binding in seam.

13. Mark center of a 15-inch length of ribbon. Mark 3¾ inches on either side of center referring to Figure 6a.

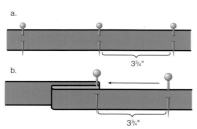

Figure 6

14. Fold ribbon at 3¾-inch marks to center back, referring to Figure 6b, and pin in place.

15. Gather stitch across width of bow at center. Pull threads to loosely gather. Tie thread ends to secure.

16. Fold finished edges of 3-inch ribbon piece to meet at center back forming a ½ x 3-inch strip.

17. Wrap 3-inch ribbon piece around folded bow center covering center pleat. Fold under top raw edge and hand-stitch together to complete bow (Figure 7). Trim bow ends into a V shape and seal with seam sealant.

Figure 7

18. Hand-stitch bows onto top straps over hook-and-loop stitching. ▪

Soothe It

Fill different-size shapes with raw rice to make a soothing hot or cold wrap for shoulders and neck, and a mask for eyes and sinuses. Warm the wrap and mask in the microwave or cool in the freezer. Add aromatic dried herbs to the rice to enjoy a mini aromatherapy treatment.

Finished Sizes
Neck/shoulder wrap: 5 x 21 inches
Eye mask: 4½ x 10 inches

Materials
- 5-inch-square green
- 2 coordinating fat quarters
- 18 x 22-inch piece light- to medium-weight fusible batting
- 8½ x 11-inch piece paper-backed fusible web
- ¼ yard ⅜-inch-wide black grosgrain ribbon
- 3 cups raw long grain rice
- Stiff paper or lightweight cardboard
- Walking foot with quilting bar
- Clover Large Flower Yo-Yo Maker (optional)
- Basic sewing supplies and equipment

Fabric Preparation & Cutting
1. Following manufacturer's instructions, fuse light-to medium-weight fusible batting to wrong side of one fat quarter.

2. Mark a horizontal or angled line at center of fused fat quarter.

3. Quilt the fused fat quarter by stitching 1½ inches apart across the fat quarter, using the marked line as a starting point and following the walking foot instructions for using the quilting bar for channel quilting (Figure 1).

Figure 1

4. Cut two 5½ x 22-inch rectangles for the neck/shoulder wrap and one 7 x 22-inch rectangle for the eye mask from the quilted fat quarter.

Preparing Appliqué Shapes
1. Trace the flower, flower center and two leaves using patterns on page 43, approximately ½ inch apart onto the paper side of the paper-backed fusible web. Cut out shapes, leaving a margin around each.

2. Follow manufacturer's instructions to fuse flower and flower center appliqué shapes to the wrong side of the unquilted fat quarter. Fuse leaf shapes to the wrong side of the green square.

3. Cut out the shapes on the traced lines. Set aside.

4. Set aside fabric remnants for Eye Mask yo yo embellishments.

Neck/Shoulder Wrap
Assembly
Use ¼-inch seam allowance and stitch right sides together unless otherwise indicated. Use a short stitch length so that the rice does not work out of the seam during use.

1. Layer, center and fuse the appliqué shapes to the center of one 5½ x 22-inch quilted rectangle referring to manufacturer's instructions and project photo.

2. Machine-stitch around the edges of each appliqué shape using a blanket stitch as shown in Figure 2.

Figure 2

3. Stitch 5½ x 22-inch quilted rectangles right sides together, leaving a 3-inch opening in one short end for filling and turning.

4. Trim corners, turn right side out, gently pushing out corners. Turn opening seam allowance to inside of rectangle and press all edges flat.

5. Make a funnel by rolling paper or cardboard into a tube; insert tube into opening in wrap and fill it between ⅓ and ½ full of raw long grain rice (Figure 3). Do not overfill. You want the bag to contour to the shape of your neck/shoulders. *Note: Add dried herbs to the rice for an aromatic wrap referring to Adding Dried Herbs to Wraps or Masks.*

Figure 3

Adding Dried Herbs to Wrap or Mask

To make the wrap or mask aromatic, add ½ to 1 teaspoon of a dried herb to the raw rice when filling the wrap or mask. Shake or stir the rice and herb to mix well.

In aromatherapy, dried lavender flowers, lemon thyme and rosemary are good choices to relieve stress and promote relaxation. Heating the wrap or mask will release both the herbal aroma and their essential oils.

6. Pin opening closed matching pressed edges of seam. Topstitch ⅛ inch around all sides of rectangle, gently moving the rice away from the stitching area as you stitch. *Note: Remember, use a shorter stitch length than usual to ensure the rice will not work out of the seam.*

Tip

Add a card to your gift with instructions for warming or cooling the wrap or mask:

*Need heat? Warm the wrap or mask in the microwave for 1–2 minutes. (**Note:** Time will vary with microwave. Test temperature before applying to skin.)*

Need cold? Put the wrap or mask in the freezer for at least 1 hour.

Eye Mask

Assembly

Use ¼-inch seam allowance and stitch right sides together unless otherwise indicated. Use a short stitch length so that the rice does not work out of the seam during use.

1. Fold the 7 x 22-inch quilted rectangle in half, right sides together lengthwise. Center Eye Mask pattern, on page 44, on folded rectangle and cut two eye masks. Transfer all pattern markings to fabric.

2. Stitch around Eye Mask, leaving an opening between squares at mask top. Turn right side out through opening. Clip curves as necessary to have smooth curves being careful not to clip through seam. Press seam allowance of opening to inside.

3. Cut two 6-inch circles from unquilted fat quarter remnants. Make two yo-yos following yo-yo maker instructions or referring to Making Yo-Yos.

4. Cut two 4-inch pieces of grosgrain ribbon. Fold each piece in half as shown in Figure 4. Hand-stitch one folded ribbon to the solid back of each yo-yo, again referring to Figure 4.

Figure 4

5. Hand-stitch yo-yos to one side of mask referring to project photo.

6. Fill mask approximately ⅓ to ½ full with raw rice referring to step 5 and Figure 3 of Neck/Shoulder Wrap Assembly instructions.

7. Pin and stitch opening closed, matching pressed edges of seam referring to step 6 of Neck/Shoulder Wrap. **Note:** *Remember, use a shorter stitch length than usual to ensure the rice will not work out of the seam.* ■

Making Yo-Yos

Using these simple instructions, you can make these easy floral-like embellishments for any sewing project.

1. *Cut a circle the size indicated in Cutting or Assembly instructions.*

2. *Finger-press ¼ inch around the circle's outer edge to the wrong side. Hand-stitch a line of gathering stitches in place around the circle taking a backstitch at the beginning to secure the thread as shown in Figure A.*

Figure A

3. *Gently pull the thread, tightly gathering the outer edge toward the center of the circle referring again to Figure A.*

4. *Knot the thread ends to secure the gathered edge and trim.*

5. *Flatten the circle with the gathered edge on the right side to complete the yo-yo as shown in Figure A.*

6. *Embellish and hand-stitch the completed yo-yo to the project as indicated in Assembly instructions.*

Buff It

Gently exfoliate and buff your skin to bring out your natural, healthy glow with this bath mitt.

Finished Size
6 x 9 inches

Materials
- 2 coordinating fat quarters A and B
- 1 coordinating terry-cloth washcloth or 11-inch square terry cloth
- 18-inch square polyester-covered foam
- 4 inches ⅜-inch-wide grosgrain ribbon or nylon cord
- ½ yard ⅝-inch-wide grosgrain ribbon
- 1½-inch flat flower button
- ½-inch flat star button
- Coordinating embroidery floss
- Fabric basting spray
- Seam sealant
- Basic sewing supplies and equipment

Cutting

From fat quarter A:
- Cut two 7-inch squares and one 11-inch square.

From fat quarter B:
- Cut 2¾-inch-wide bias strips to make 32 inches of bias binding.

From polyester-covered foam:
- Cut one 7-inch square and one 11-inch square.

Assembly
Use ¼-inch seam allowance and stitch right sides together unless otherwise indicated.

1. Trace Bottom pattern given on page 46 onto right side of 11-inch fat quarter A square with fabric marker.

2. Spray one side of the 11-inch square of polyester-covered foam with basting spray. Smooth the wrong side of terry-cloth washcloth or square centered on sprayed side.

3. Flip basted pieces over and spray opposite side of polyester-covered foam. Smooth wrong side of the marked fat quarter A square onto foam (Figure 1).

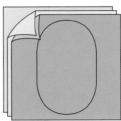

Figure 1

4. Set your machine for a long stitch length, about 5–6 stitches per inch, and stitch through all layers close to the traced line. Cut out close to stitching. *Note: Check your machine manual for information on changing stitch lengths.*

5. Trace Top pattern on page 45 onto right side of one 7-inch fat quarter A square. Layer, baste and stitch 7-inch polyester-covered foam between 7-inch A squares referring to steps 2–4.

6. Stitch ends of bias strips together with angled seam to make a strip at least 32 inches long (Figure 2).

Figure 2

7. Press seams open. Fold bias strip in half wrong sides together lengthwise and press to make bias binding.

8. Cut 6-inch length of bias binding. Align and stitch long raw edges of binding along straight edge of top piece (Figure 3a).

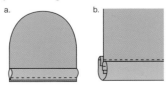

Figure 3

Sugar Scrub
Skin Treatment

Mix together and store in covered jar:

1 cup sugar

½ cup light olive or almond oil

1 or 2 drops your favorite essential oil

To use: Apply small amount to Buff
It bath mitt and gently scrub. Rinse
with warm water and dry.

9. Turn bias binding to wrong side, overlapping first stitching, and pin. Stitch-in-the-ditch or topstitch along binding seam on right side to secure (Figure 3b).

Tip

Basting thick layers of fabric and foam or batting together with pins can be a problem. Basting tape is sticky on both sides and is available in ¼-inch or ½-inch widths, just wide enough to keep a seam allowance in place.

Apply the tape between the layers and along the raw edges, pressing to hold. Stitch through all layers.

10. Cut 6-inch length of grosgrain ribbon. Position and topstitch ribbon next to binding edge on right side of top piece referring to photo.

11. Position and pin top piece on fat quarter A side of bottom piece, matching rounded edges (Figure 4). Baste together bath mitt layers and trim edges even if necessary.

Figure 4

12. Unfold one binding end and fold ¼ inch to wrong side on one short end. Press and refold lengthwise.

13. Position the binding around the right or fat quarter A side of the basted bath mitt layers matching raw edges and beginning with folded short end at one side (Figure 5).

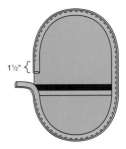

1½"

Figure 5

14. Begin stitching 1½ inches away from folded short end of binding and stopping stitching approximately 2 inches from folded short end of binding referring again to Figure 5. Remove from machine.

15. Trim end of binding so that it overlaps the folded beginning end ¼ inch referring to Figure 6. Insert trimmed end inside folded end and continue stitching.

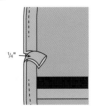

¼"

Figure 6

16. Fold binding to back or terry-cloth side of stitched bath mitt layers and pin, overlapping first stitching. Stitch-in-the-ditch or topstitch along binding edge on front side to secure.

17. If using ribbon to make hanging loop, fold in half right sides together lengthwise and stitch together. Loop folded ribbon or cord over itself (Figure 7). Seal ends with seam sealant.

Figure 7

18. Center ribbon loop on the reverse side at top edge of Buff It bath mitt, referring to photo for placement. Stitch over binding stitching to secure ribbon/cord ends.

19. Layer 1½-inch and ½-inch buttons onto folded 12-inch length of ribbon referring to photo for placement. Stitch buttons to ribbon using embroidery floss. Seal ends of ribbon with seam sealant. Hand-tack to bath mitt at top front edge. ■

Scrunch It

Combine the Scrunch It, the Buff It mitt and a fragrant body wash and you've got a great gift combo that is sure to relax away the day's stress.

Materials
- ¾ yard 72-inch-wide nylon netting
- ⅔ yard ³⁄₁₆-inch home decor nylon cord or narrow ribbon
- Rubber band
- Basic sewing supplies and equipment

Cutting

From nylon netting:
- Cut five 7 x 36-inch strips.

Assembly

1. Stack nylon netting strips. Fold strip stack into 1-inch pleats along the width (Figure 1). Place a pin at center of strip stack to hold pleats together.

Figure 1

2. Wrap together at center with a rubber band, removing pin as you wrap.

3. Tie nylon cord or ribbon tightly around center with square knot (Figure 2).

Figure 2

4. Tie knots close to each end of cord. If using ribbon, treat ends with seam sealant.

5. Tie loose ends of cord or ribbon together with a square knot to form a hanging loop.

6. Gently pull apart the net layers to fluff the puff ball. ■

Cover It

Warm and comfy, this small blanket is light enough to tuck into the Carry It and heavy enough to take the chill out of any airplane or long car ride. The large pocket is handy for a favorite book.

Finished Size
- 35 x 42 inches

Materials
- 2 coordinating 44/45-inch-wide lightweight woven prints or solids:
  - 1 yard each of fabric A and B
- 1 coordinating fat quarter
- 18 x 22-inch piece light- to medium-weight fusible batting
- 1 yard ¾-inch-wide ribbon (optional)
- Safety pins
- Walking foot with quilting bar (optional)
- Basic sewing supplies and equipment

Cutting

From fabric A:
- Cut one 36-inch by fabric width blanket front.

From fabric B:
- Cut one 36-inch by fabric width blanket back.

From coordinating fat quarter:
- Fold fat quarter in half across 18-inch width. Cut two pockets on fold using pattern provided on page 47, referring to Figure 1.

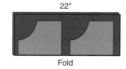

22"

Fold

Figure 1

From fusible batting:
- Fold batting in half across 18-inch width. Cut one pocket on fold using pattern provided on page 47.

Assembly
Use ¼-inch seam allowance and stitch right sides together unless otherwise indicated.

1. Place both blanket pieces right sides together. Trim selvages and square up pieces to 35 x 42 inches.

2. Pin and stitch blanket pieces together along long sides first and then the short sides. Leave a 6-inch opening for turning at center of last side stitched. *Note: Stop after stitching each side and check that the pieces are still square. Using a walking foot when stitching long seams helps keep the fabrics even.*

3. Trim corners at an angle and turn right side out, gently pushing corners out.

4. Turn seam allowance of opening to inside and press all seam edges flat.

5. Topstitch around blanket ⅛-inch from edges, stitching the opening closed.

6. Mark parallel stitching lines approximately 6 inches apart on blanket back or front with removable fabric marker or chalk (Figure 2). *Note: Or you could choose to mark horizontal, vertical or angled stitching lines.* Pin layers together with safety pins approximately every 3 inches, again referring to Figure 2.

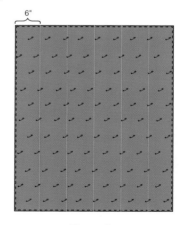

6"

Figure 2

7. Stitch layers together along marked stitching lines, removing safety pins as you stitch.

8. Choose one pocket piece as pocket and one as lining. Follow manufacturer's instructions and fuse pocket batting to wrong side of pocket.

9. Stitch fused pocket and lining pieces right sides together, leaving a 2-inch opening at bottom edge for turning.

10. Trim corners at an angle; clip curves and turn right side out, gently pushing corners out.

11. Turn seam allowance of opening to inside and press all seam edges flat.

12. Topstitch using a straight stitch or decorative machine stitch around the pocket curved edges (Figure 3). *Note: See Pocket Embellishment Option to add ribbon trim.*

Figure 3

13. Position and pin completed pocket 18 inches from top and 10 inches from side edges of blanket front (Figure 4).

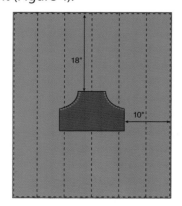

Figure 4

14. Edgestitch top, straight sides and bottom of pocket, leaving curved sides unstitched to finish blanket. ∎

Pocket Embellishment Option

Embellish the blanket pocket top and bottom edges with ribbon or other flat trim instead of, or in addition to, the decorative machine stitching along the curved edges.

• Cut one each 15½-inch and 7½-inch lengths of ribbon.

• Position and pin ribbon lengths ⅜ inch from completed pocket front top and bottom referring to pocket pattern and Figure A. Fold ribbon ends to back side of pocket and pin to hold.

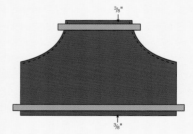

Figure A

• Edgestitch ribbon in place.

• Attach embellished pocket to blanket following Assembly steps 13 and 14.

Carry It

This bag was designed to hold the Cover It blanket for airline or car travel. There is also an inner pocket for an iPad®, tablet or other mobile device.

Finished Size
• Approximately 10 x 16 inches

Materials
• ⅝ yard each coordinating large and small prints
• 18 x 22-inch piece light- to medium-weight fusible batting
• 1 yard ⅝-inch-wide grosgrain ribbon or twill tape
• 3 (1-inch) flat buttons
• 5 (¾-inch) coordinating flat buttons
• Coordinating embroidery floss
• Seam sealant
• Basic sewing supplies and equipment

Cutting

From large print:
• Cut one 18 by fabric width rectangle; subcut one 18 x 22-inch piece for bag body.

From small print:
• Cut one 2-inch by fabric width strip; subcut one 2 x 22-inch strip for tie casing.
• Cut one 16-inch by fabric width rectangle; subcut one 16 x 22-inch rectangle for inside pocket.

From fusible batting:
• Cut one 1 x 22-inch strip for tie casing.
• Cut one 8 x 22-inch rectangle for pocket.

Assembly
Use ¼-inch seam allowance and stitch right sides together unless otherwise indicated.

1. Press ¼ inch fabric to wrong side along 22-inch side of bag body. Fold again 1 inch to wrong side to make bag top hem. Press and edgestitch along first fold referring to Figure 1.

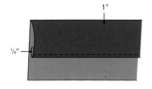

Figure 1

2. Fuse 1 x 22-inch fusible batting centered on wrong side of 2 x 22-inch small print tie casing. Trim fused casing to 21 inches long.

3. Fold both short ends of fused casing ¼ inch to wrong side; press. Fold lengthwise raw edges of bag tie casing over fused batting and press (Figure 2).

Figure 2

4. Topstitch casing short ends ⅛ inch from pressed edge.

5. Place casing ¾ inch down from bag body top and ¾ inch in from sides and edgestitch along both long sides of casing leaving ends open (Figure 3). Set aside.

Figure 3

6. Fuse 8 x 22-inch fusible batting to wrong side of bottom half of 16 x 22-inch inside pocket matching raw edges.

7. Fold top half of inside pocket over the fusible batting and edgestitch along fold. Fold and press inside pocket in half lengthwise to mark center.

8. Position inside pocket on lower part of wrong side of bag body matching raw edges; machine-baste sides and bottom of inside pocket to bag body (Figure 4).

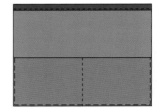

Figure 4

9. Stitch along pressed centerline of inside pocket dividing the pocket into two sections, referring again to Figure 4.

10. To make a French seam for bag side and bottom seams, fold completed bag body wrong sides together and stitch a ⅛-inch seam along sides and bottom. Turn bag wrong side out and press seams flat.

11. With right sides together, stitch a ¼-inch seam along sides and bottom of bag. Turn right side out and press.

12. Stitch buttons to casing evenly spaced on one side referring to the photo. *Note: Stack ¾-inch buttons on 1-inch buttons, and using six-strand embroidery floss, stitch through the first hole from the top leaving a long tail; then take a stitch through the casing fabric only and back up through the second buttonhole. Make sure not to catch the bag fabric in the stitch. Tie the embroidery floss in a square knot on top of the buttons.*

13. Attach a safety pin to one end of the grosgrain ribbon or twill tape and thread through the casing leaving tails on either end of casing.

14. Trim ribbon or twill to desired length and tie knot in both ends. Seal ends with seam sealant. Stitch remaining ¾-inch buttons below knots. ■

Hang It

This padded hanger is so cute that you may not want to cover it with clothes! Hang clothes over this padded hanger cover to eliminate hanger lines or under the padded cover for dust protection.

Finished Size
- Fits standard 17-inch-wide plastic hangers

Materials
- 1 fat quarter coordinating solid color A
- 2 matching fat quarters print B
- 18 x 22-inch piece light- to medium-weight fusible batting
- ⅔ yard jumbo rickrack
- Sew-on 6mm pearls or beads
- Walking foot with quilting bar (optional)
- Basic sewing supplies and equipment

Preparing Cover Fabric
1. Follow manufacturer's instructions to apply fusible batting to wrong side of fat quarter A.

2. Mark 45-degree diagonal lines 1½ inches apart in one direction on right side of A with fabric marker (Figure 1).

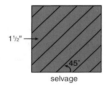

Figure 1

3. Stitch on the marked lines to quilt the entire fused A fat quarter.

Cutting

From quilted A fat quarter:
- Fold in half, right sides together, to make an 11 x 18-inch rectangle. Place Cover pattern from pattern insert on fold and cut two referring to Cutting Chart 1. Transfer all pattern marks to fabric.

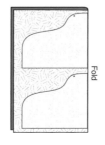

Cutting Chart 1

From matching B fat quarters:
- Fold one fat quarter in half, right sides together, to make an 11 x 18-inch rectangle. Place Cover pattern on fold and cut two referring to Cutting Chart 2.

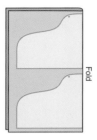

Cutting Chart 2

- Repeat with second fat quarter and Cover Bodice pattern from pattern insert, referring to Cutting Chart 3.

Cutting Chart 3

Assembly
Use ¼-inch seam allowance and stitch right sides together unless otherwise indicated.

1. Pin and stitch bodice pieces right sides together on curved edges only. Clip curves referring to Figure 2.

Figure 2

2. Turn right sides out and press flat.

3. Position stitched bodice on right side of one cover for front, matching bottom straight edges.

4. Tuck rickrack under the bodice curved edge; pin in place (Figure 3). Edgestitch bodice curved edge to secure and baste straight edges.

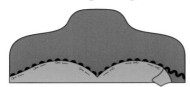

Figure 3

5. Position and pin approximately 9 inches of remaining rickrack on neckline of front cover referring to Figure 4. Stitch through center of rickrack to secure. Trim rickrack ends even with cover.

Figure 4

6. Turn ¼ inch to wrong side of each cover piece at neck between square markings, tapering to squares at top of cover, making a semicircular hem (Figure 5). Sew one or two lines of stitching along the hem edge.

Figure 5

Tip

Be sure to knot your thread before and after adding each pearl or bead to any item that will see even moderate use.

If a pearl or bead should fall off the item, you will not lose the whole string because of the extra knots.

7. Stitch cover front and back right sides together along both curved sides matching raw edges and square markings (Figure 6). Clip curves referring again to Figure 6 and turn right side out.

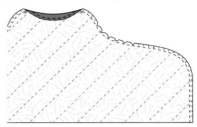

Figure 6

8. Repeat with fat quarter B Cover pieces for lining. Do not turn right side out.

9. Slip the lining over the quilted cover matching side seams and straight bottom edges right sides together. Pin and stitch straight bottom edges. *Note: When matching side seams, pin seam allowances in opposite directions referring to Figure 7.*

Figure 7

10. Turn right side out through top opening and press flat. Topstitch ⅛ inch from bottom edge.

11. Hand-stitch the cover and lining together at the top opening.

12. Hand-stitch pearls or beads to the rickrack "necklace" and the V of the bodice, referring to the project photo. ■

Protect It

Keep garments safe in this easy-to-make garment bag.
Size is adjustable to fit your needs.

Finished Size
42 x 22 inches

Making Different-Size Garment Bags

A 42-inch-long garment bag is a suit-length bag. It will cover blouses, shirts, men's and women's suits, short coats and sweaters.

For a dress-length (52-inch-long) garment bag, purchase 2 yards fabric. Cut four 3 x 42-inch strips for front binding and one 53-inch by fabric width rectangle for garment bag referring to cutting instructions.

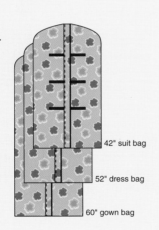

For a gown-length (60-inch-long) garment bag, purchase 2⅛ yards fabric. Cut four 3 x 42-inch strips for front binding and one 61-inch by fabric width rectangle for garment bag referring to cutting instructions.

Complete all assembly instructions as written except sew the binding strips together with angled seams and then cut two strips the length of the bag rectangle, either 53 inches for dress length or 61 inches for gown length.

Materials
- 1½ yards 44/45-inch-wide woven fabric
- 1¼ yards ⅝-inch-wide coordinating grosgrain ribbon
- Basic sewing supplies and equipment

Cutting

From woven fabric:
- Cut two 3 x 42-inch strips for front binding.
- Cut one 42-inch by fabric width rectangle for garment bag. Carefully trim the selvages from the fabric, making sure edges are straight.

From grosgrain ribbon:
- Cut six 7-inch-long pieces for bag ties.

Assembly
Use ¼-inch seam allowance and stitch right sides together unless otherwise indicated.

1. Fold garment bag rectangle in half lengthwise, wrong sides together and press to mark center.

2. Unfold and cut rectangle in half along pressed centerline.

3. Fold both pieces of the garment bag rectangle in half lengthwise, wrong sides together (Figure 1).

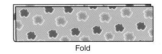

Fold

Figure 1

4. To trim end of garment bag piece, position top trimming pattern from pattern insert on fold as shown in Figure 2 and trim around curved edge of pattern. Transfer all pattern markings to fabric. Repeat with second garment bag piece. Set aside one piece for garment bag back.

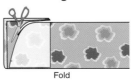

Fold

Figure 2

5. Cut lengthwise along the folded edge of one trimmed garment bag piece to make two garment bag fronts.

Tip

Raw edges usually fray or ravel when washed. If using a standard sewing machine, take the time to finish all raw edges of the garment bag rectangle before beginning assembly. Stitch along the raw edges of the garment bag rectangle with a zigzag or overedge stitch before stitching your seams.

If using a serger, simply use a three- or four-thread overlock stitch to sew the garment bag seams.

---

6. Fold and press front binding strips in half lengthwise, wrong sides together. Fold and press again ¼ inch to wrong side along one length of each binding strip (Figure 3).

Figure 3

7. Pin and stitch right side of binding raw edge to wrong side of center front edge of one garment bag front (Figure 4). Repeat on second front.

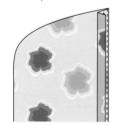

Figure 4

8. Pin three ribbon lengths along the center front edge of each garment bag front, right sides together, 11 inches from top and spaced 10 inches apart referring to Figure 5. Baste ribbon in place inside seam line.

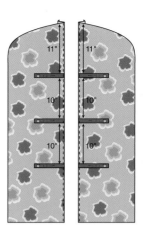

Figure 5

9. Turn and pin folded edge of binding to right side of garment bag front placing folded edge over stitching line and ribbon ends. Edgestitch along folded binding edge (Figure 6). Repeat on second front panel.

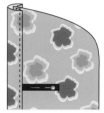

Figure 6

10. Overlap and pin garment bag fronts, right over left (Figure 7), making sure the fronts are the same width as the back; machine- or hand-baste front edges together.

Figure 7

11. Turn ¼ inch to wrong side between the squares on front and back top edges. Topstitch two rows of stitching along the turned edges.

12. Layer and pin basted fronts and back right sides together matching squares and all raw edges.

13. Stitch from square to square around the garment bag side and bottom edges leaving open at top between squares. Turn right side out.

14. Press flat and topstitch completely around outside. ■

Bandage It

Be ready for any small emergency. Tuck adhesive bandages, alcohol wipes, hand sanitizer, cotton swabs and even needle and thread into this small tote.

Finished Size
4 x 6 inches

Materials
- Scrap tan tonal
- 1 fat quarter red dot print
- ¼ yard cotton duck solid
- 5 x 14-inch piece lightweight fusible batting
- 2 x 9-inch piece paper-backed fusible web
- 7-inch polyester zipper
- 6-inch length ⅛- to ⅜-inch-wide ribbon
- Fabric basting spray
- Seam sealant
- Sewing machine feet (optional)
    walking foot
    embroidery foot
    zipper foot
- Basic sewing supplies and equipment

Cutting

From cotton duck:
- Cut two 5 x 7-inch rectangles for outer tote.

From red dot print:
- Cut two 5 x 7-inch rectangles for tote lining.

From lightweight fusible batting:
- Cut two 5 x 7-inch rectangles.

Assembly
Use ¼-inch seam allowance and stitch right sides together unless otherwise indicated.

1. Trace one each Bandage and Bandage Pad pattern from pattern insert ½ inch apart on paper side of paper-backed fusible web. Cut out shapes leaving margin around each.

2. Fuse bandage on wrong side of tan tonal following manufacturer's instructions. Cut out on traced lines.

3. Fuse bandage pad to wrong side of red dot print scrap and cut out on traced lines.

4. Remove paper backing and fuse bandage to one of the outer tote rectangles centered diagonally at least ¼ inch from edges (Figure 1).

Figure 1

5. Fuse bandage pad centered on the bandage referring again to Figure 1.

6. Machine-stitch around all edges with a zigzag or blanket stitch (Figure 2).

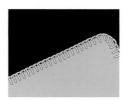

Figure 2

7. Fuse batting to wrong sides of both outer tote rectangles following manufacturer's instructions.

8. Center and pin zipper right sides together on the appliquéd outer tote rectangle matching zipper tape edge to rectangle edge (Figure 3).

Figure 3

9. Unzip zipper halfway. Starting at open end of zipper, machine-baste a scant ¼ inch from tape edge to zipper pull (Figure 4a). Remove from machine and close zipper.

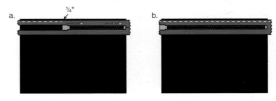

Figure 4

Tip

Zippers don't have to be the same color of the fabric they are being sewn into. Add a splash of color to any project, like totes or bags, where the zipper teeth and tape will show by using a zipper that contrasts or complements the fabric.

It's an Eazy Peazy color pop!

10. Return to machine and continue basting zipper in place, referring to Figure 4b.

11. Position and pin a lining rectangle right side down with zipper between outer tote and lining, matching zipper tape and outer tote edges. Refer to

Laminate Your Tote

Purchase laminated fabric or treat your fabric with iron-on vinyl following the manufacturer's instructions to easily create a liquid-resistant tote. Follow these simple tips to work with laminated fabrics.

• Needle and pin holes will show on laminated fabrics or vinyl. Avoid ripping seams and use self-adhesive, double-sided basting tape instead of pins.

• For fabrics treated with iron-on vinyl, follow the manufacturer's directions for application and ironing. Always use a protective paper between the vinyl and your iron.

• Do not touch a hot iron to the laminated side of the fabric. For best results, finger-press seams and edges flat. If pressing is necessary, use an iron on the lowest setting and press on the wrong side of the laminated fabric only using a press cloth.

• Finger-press seam allowances to one side and stitch in place instead of pressing them open. This increases the water resistance of the finished project.

• Use a sharp size 12 needle in your machine. A Teflon presser foot is helpful when sewing on these types of fabrics. It will glide over the fabrics.

steps 9 and 10, and Figure 5 to stitch lining in place ¼-inch from zipper tape edge.

Figure 5

12. Carefully press the lining and outer tote rectangles away from the zipper teeth. With basting spray, spray the wrong side of the lining rectangle and then smooth over the wrong side of the outer tote rectangle. Trim lining to match outer tote if necessary.

13. Topstitch ⅛ inch from zipper seam as shown in Figure 6.

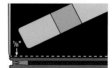

Figure 6

14. Repeat steps 8–13 with remaining outer tote and lining rectangles on opposite side of zipper (Figure 7).

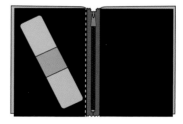

Figure 7

15. Unzip zipper halfway. Match raw edges of tote with outer tote right sides together and pin.

16. Stitch sides and bottom of tote as shown in Figure 8. Finish raw edges with zigzag or overedge stitch. ***Note:*** *Be sure to stitch over the ends of the zipper to secure.*

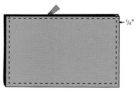

Figure 8

17. Box tote corners by matching the side and bottom seams; press seam allowances in opposite directions. Stitch across the corner, approximately ½-inch from corner triangle tip referring to Figure 9.

Figure 9

18. Turn tote right side out through open zipper.

19. Thread ribbon through zipper pull and tie in a square knot; trim ends if necessary. Seal ends of ribbon with seam sealant. ■

Pattern Templates

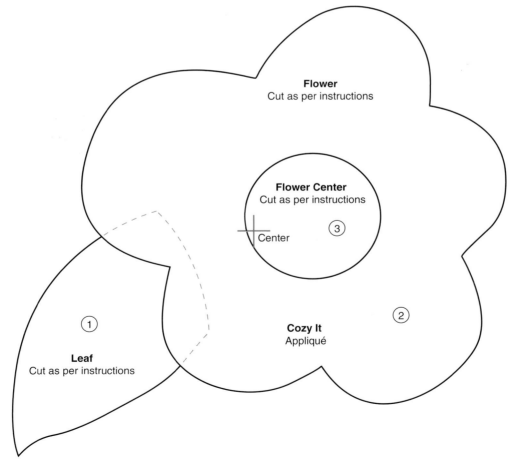

Flower
Cut as per instructions

Flower Center
Cut as per instructions

Center ③

Cozy It
Appliqué ②

Leaf
Cut as per instructions ①

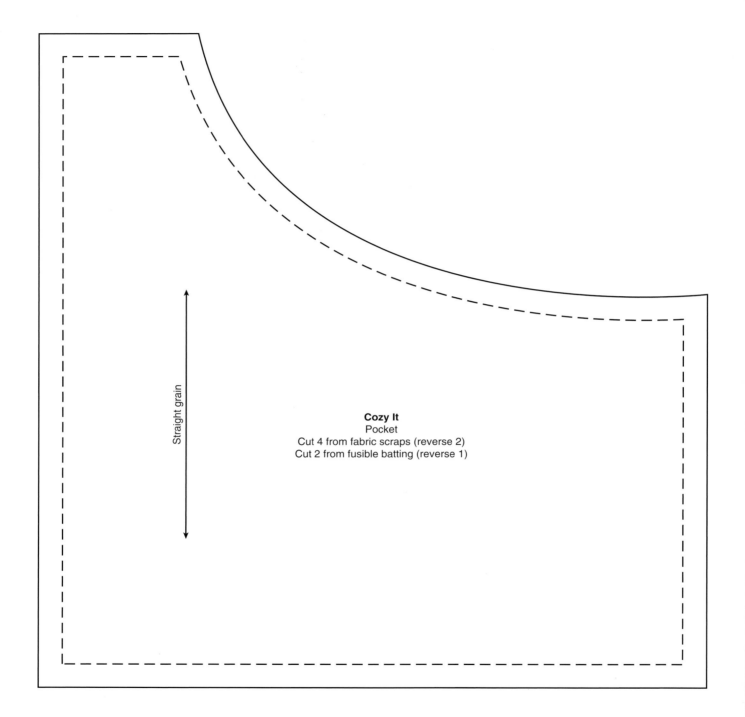

Cozy It
Pocket
Cut 4 from fabric scraps (reverse 2)
Cut 2 from fusible batting (reverse 1)

Straight grain

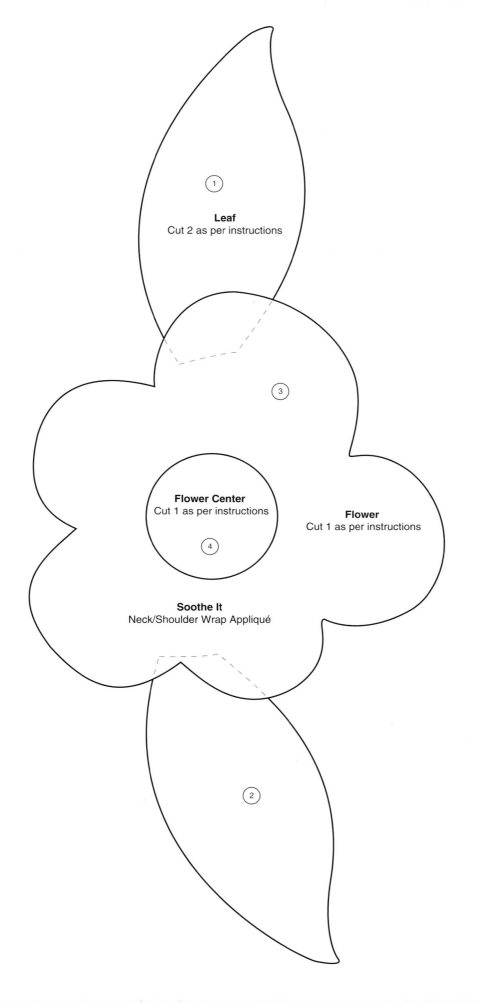

Leaf
Cut 2 as per instructions

Flower Center
Cut 1 as per instructions

Flower
Cut 1 as per instructions

Soothe It
Neck/Shoulder Wrap Appliqué

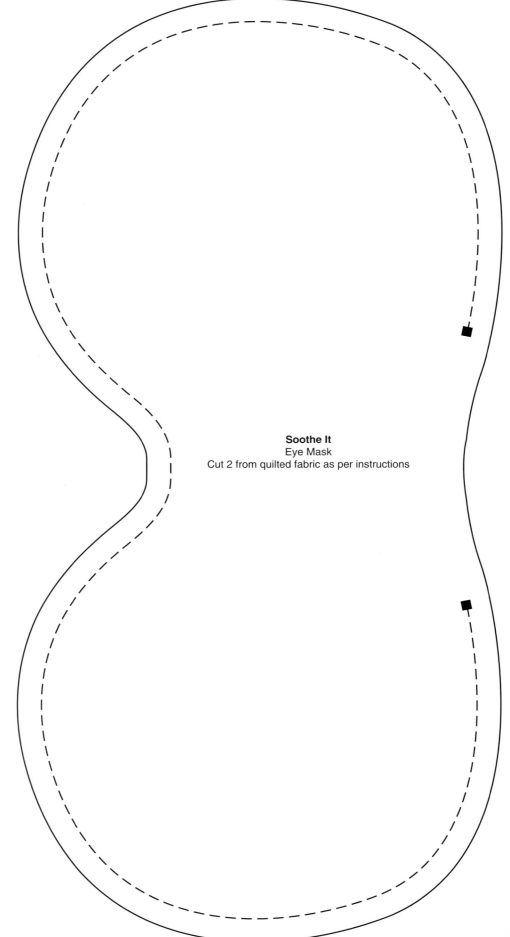

Soothe It
Eye Mask
Cut 2 from quilted fabric as per instructions

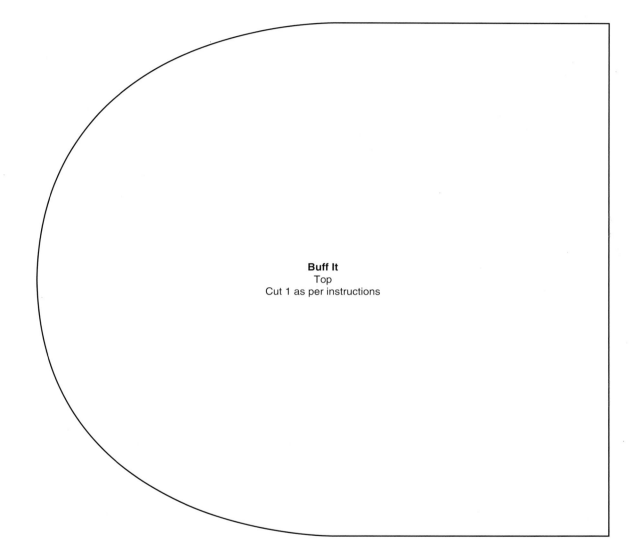

Buff It
Top
Cut 1 as per instructions

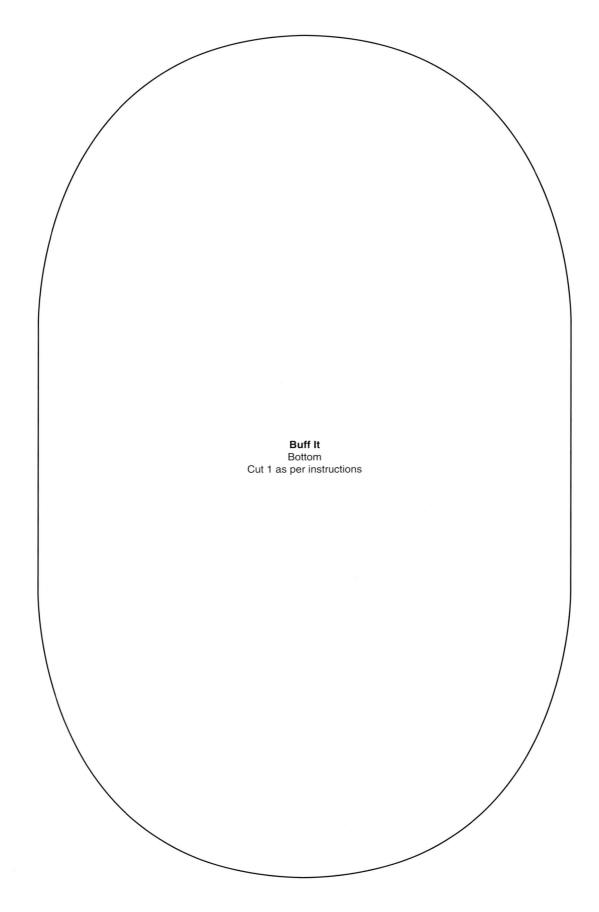

Buff It
Bottom
Cut 1 as per instructions

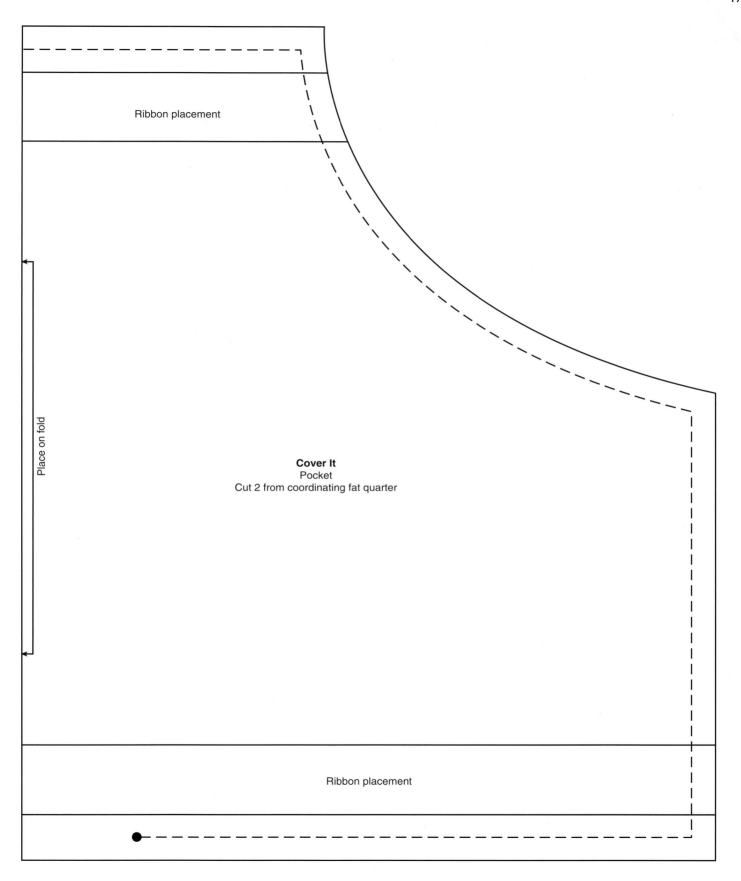

Ribbon placement

Place on fold

Cover It
Pocket
Cut 2 from coordinating fat quarter

Ribbon placement

Fabric & Supplies

The following materials were used to construct the projects in this book and are available from the companies listed.

Light fusible batting, sew-in batting, CRAF-TEX heavy-weight interfacing and polyester-covered foam stabilizer all from Bosal (www.bosalonline.com)

Pattern transfer materials available through Annie's Quilt & Sew (AnniesCatalog.com): Swedish tracing paper, pattern tracing paper and Do Sew tracing material by Stretch & Sew

KK 2000™ temporary spray fabric adhesive and Tear-Easy™ stabilizer from Sulky® (www.sulky.com)

The designer used the following fabric collections in the listed projects:

Cozy It, page 10
Fabulous Felines collection by Laurel Burch for Clothworks (www.clothworkstextiles.com)

Hang It, page 32; Protect It, page 35; Stow It, page 7
Bora-Bora Collection from Blank Fabrics (www.blankquilting.com)

Buff It, page 22; Carry It, page 29; Cover It, page 26; Scuff It, page 14
Birds and Berries collection from Moda Fabrics (www.unitednotions.com)

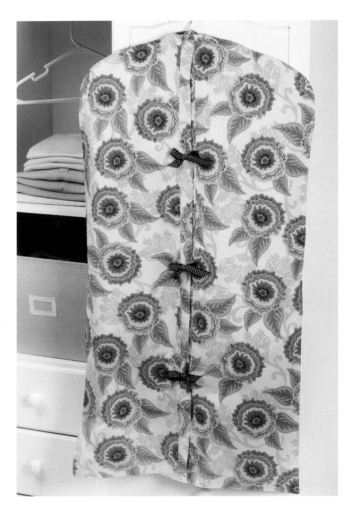

Annie's® *Eazy Peazy Gifts* is published by Annie's, 306 East Parr Road, Berne, IN 46711. Printed in USA. Copyright © 2013 Annie's. All rights reserved. This publication may not be reproduced in part or in whole without written permission from the publisher.

RETAIL STORES: If you would like to carry this pattern book or any other Annie's publications, visit AnniesWSL.com.

Every effort has been made to ensure that the instructions in this pattern book are complete and accurate. We cannot, however, take responsibility for human error, typographical mistakes or variations in individual work. Please visit AnniesCustomerCare.com to check for pattern updates.

ISBN: 978-1-59635-637-5

2 3 4 5 6 7 8 9